D0792175

W6-BBF-346

FIRE BREATHING, SWORD SWALLOWING, AND OTHER DEATH-DEFYING

CIRCUS SCIENCE

by WIL MARA

Consultant:
Vesal Dini, PhD in Physics
Postdoctoral Scholar at
Tufts University
Center for Engineering Education Outreach
Medford, Massachusetts

CAPSTONE PRESS
a capstone imprint

Edge Books are published by Capstone Press,
1710 Roe Crest Drive, North Mankato, Minnesota 56003
www.mycapstone.com

Copyright ©2018 by Capstone Press, a Capstone imprint. All rights reserved.
No part of this publication may be reproduced in whole or in part, or stored in a retrieval system, or transmitted in any form or by any means, electronic, mechanical, photocopying, recording, or otherwise, without written permission of the publisher.

Library of Congress Cataloging-in-Publication Data
Names: Mara, Wil, author.
Title: Fire breathing, sword swallowing, and other death-defying circus
    science / by Wil Mara.
Description: North Mankato, Minnesota : Capstone Press, a Capstone imprint,
    [2017] | Series: Edge books. Circus science | Includes bibliographical
    references and index. | Audience: 4-6.
Identifiers: LCCN 2017012457|
ISBN 9781515772835 (library binding) |
ISBN 9781515772873 (eBook PDF) | I
Subjects: LCSH: Circus performers—Juvenile literature. | Circus—Juvenile
    literature.
Classification: LCC GV1817 .M37 2017 | DDC 791.3—dc23
LC record available at https://lccn.loc.gov/2017012457

Editorial Credits
Abby Colich, editor; Heidi Thompson, designer; Kelly Garvin,
media researcher; Laura Manthe, production specialist

Photo Credits
Alamy: ERIC LAFFORGUE, 16, Guy Bell, 29, PA Images, 5, REUTERS, 24-25; Getty
Images: ABDEKHAK SENNA/Staff, 6-7, Franziska Krug, 21, Neville Elder, 12, Portland
Press Herald, 23, Richard Lautens, 8, Taxi/Mike Owen, 15; Newscom: LEE CELANO/
REUTERS, 27; Shutterstock: a katz, 10-11, CHEN WS, 18, jgolby, cover

Artistic elements: Shutterstock: 21, benchart, Gun2becontinued, Igor Vitkovskiy, mik-
ser45, Milissa4like, Nimaxs, Roberto Castillo, s_maria, Supphachai Salaeman

Printed In the United States of America.
010364F17

TABLE OF CONTENTS

Death-Defying Circus Acts

Welcome to the circus! The world's most death-defying stunts are about to make you ooh, ahh, gasp, and even cringe. A man will walk across a wire 30 feet (9.1 meters) in the air. A woman held up only by her hair will spin as she hangs from a rope. Five motorcyclists will speed around the inside of a giant ball-shaped cage at tremendous speed.

How are these daring stunts possible? They all conform to the laws of nature. Physics, chemistry, anatomy, and even math can be used to describe the world's most death-defying circus acts. From sword swallowing to glass walking, there's a lot more science at work here than you probably ever realized.

DO NOT TRY THIS AT HOME

Circus acts are a blast to watch, but DO NOT try them yourself. Performers spend years training. They practice every day. Performing a circus act without the proper training and correct safety precautions could result in serious injury. Instead, simple activities that you CAN TRY are included in these pages. They will help you understand the science behind the circus. They are safe, easy, and fun!

HIGH-WIRE WALKING

The circus is about to begin! High above the center ring you see a long, thick wire stretched tightly between two poles. At one end of the wire, a circus performer slowly begins to walk across it. You hold your breath as he performs hops and turns on the wobbling wire. You breathe a sigh of relief when he makes it safely to the other end.

What keeps him from tumbling down? The tightrope walker must carefully manage something called his **center of mass**. Any everyday object has a center of mass. If you stand perfectly straight, your center of mass is located about halfway up your body. When a performer steps onto a tightrope, he must keep his center of mass balanced directly above his feet. If he leans too much one way or another, **gravity** will pull him to the ground.

center of mass—the point in an object around which its mass is evenly distributed

gravity—an attractive force that exists between any two objects, including between Earth and everything on it

⟨ DON'T TRY THIS AT HOME

⌄ TRY THIS INSTEAD

Try this experiment to see center of mass at work. Take a crisp dollar bill (not an old, wrinkly one). Fold it into a V. Balance it on its side on a table. Then balance a quarter on top of the corner edge of the V. The quarter will stay there because its center of mass is balanced evenly on the corner of the V. Now, very slowly, spread the two ends of the bill away from each other, making the V wider. If its center of mass is in the right place, the quarter will not fall off, even after the dollar bill is completely straight. If the quarter does fall off, try again.

CIRCUS FACT

Nik Wallenda set the record for the longest tightrope walk on August 11, 2015. He walked along a wire strung 10 stories in the air for 1,576 feet (480.3 meters).

HUMAN
CANNONBALLS

Boom! The blast of a huge cannon shakes your seat. But it's not a cannonball that shoots out. It's a human being! The audience gasps as they watch him fly through the air. He lands on a net on the other side of the ring. A few moments later, he stands up and waves to the audience.

How can a person survive such a blast? In a normal cannon, there is a small explosion inside the barrel. The explosion propels the cannonball out of the barrel. Fortunately, circus cannons work in a safer way. They compress, or force, air into a smaller **volume** or space. Air is full of tiny particles you can't see. As the air is compressed, the particles are pushed closer together. This causes an increase in **pressure**. The air is compressed so much that when it is given the opportunity to occupy a larger space, the particles push outward. This outward **force** is strong enough to push the person out of the cannon at great speed.

volume—the amount of space taken up by an object
pressure—a force exerted on an object over a particular amount of its surface
force—an interaction, such as a push or pull, that changes the motion of an object

DON'T TRY THIS AT HOME

TRY THIS INSTEAD

See the power of compressed air yourself. Find an empty plastic water bottle. Make sure the cap is on tight. Hold the top half of the bottle in one hand. With the other, twist the bottom half around and around. This will compress the air from the bottom half into the top. This builds up a lot of pressure. Now, aim the cap in some safe direction, away from other people or things that can break. Then twist the cap off very quickly. Did it fly away with a powerful pop? This reaction is similar to the release of compressed air that shoots a person out of a cannon.

CIRCUS FACT

When a circus cannon fires, you may see a flash of light and a cloud of smoke. That's just a special effect. It's added to make it look like a real cannon's explosion.

FLYING TRAPEZE

You're excited for the next act. You see two wires hanging from the ceiling. There's a narrow bar between them. An acrobat jumps from a high platform and grabs the bar. He swings on the bar before jumping off and into the arms of a different performer swinging from another bar. These flying trapeze artists glide back and forth through the air.

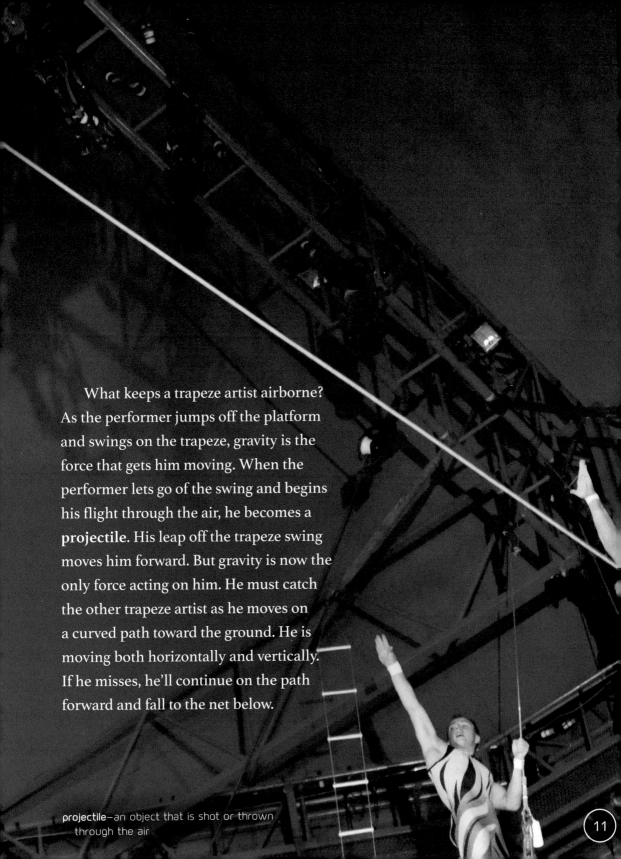

What keeps a trapeze artist airborne? As the performer jumps off the platform and swings on the trapeze, gravity is the force that gets him moving. When the performer lets go of the swing and begins his flight through the air, he becomes a **projectile.** His leap off the trapeze swing moves him forward. But gravity is now the only force acting on him. He must catch the other trapeze artist as he moves on a curved path toward the ground. He is moving both horizontally and vertically. If he misses, he'll continue on the path forward and fall to the net below.

projectile—an object that is shot or thrown through the air

SWORD SWALLOWING

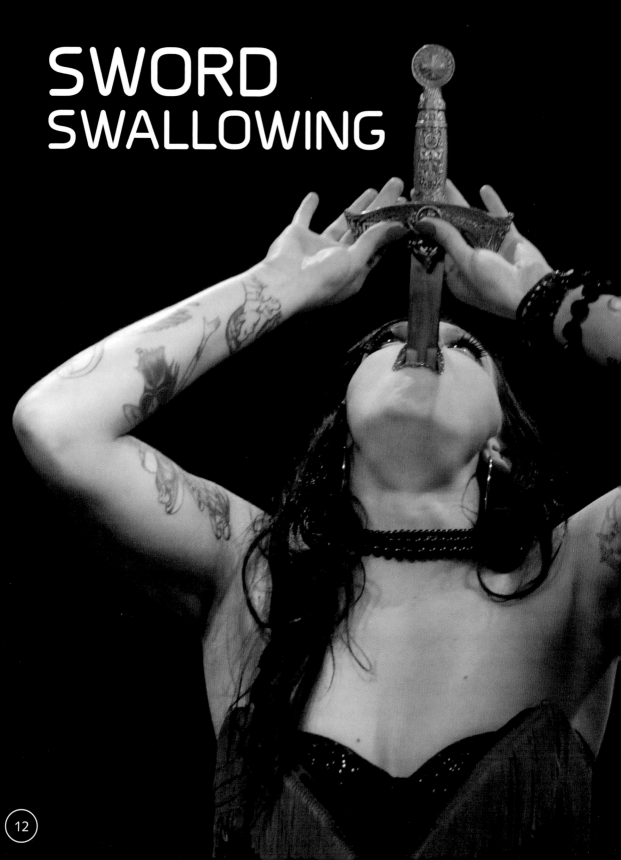

The suspense of this next act will make you gulp! A circus performer walks onto the stage. She pulls out a long, thin sword. She leans her head back, opens her mouth, and slides the sword down her throat until just the handle sticks out. Then she pulls it back up as the crowd gasps. The performer appears unhurt. Is the sword fake? No, it's very real and made of solid steel!

What's the trick to sword swallowing? Correct movement is the key. The performer practices holding her tongue down and out of the way. She learns how to move the muscles in her throat so that it is as wide as possible. The performer must slowly slide the sword as it travels through her **esophagus** toward the stomach. Moving the sword slowly helps prevent injury. She cannot make any sudden movements.

That's not all. Often, the blade of the sword isn't very sharp. Sometimes the performer puts oil on the sword's blade beforehand. The **lubricant** creates less **friction**. The blade becomes very slippery. It is much easier to slide in and out.

esophagus—the tube that carries food from the mouth to the stomach
lubricant—a slippery substance that helps the surfaces of two objects to
   easily move against each other
friction—a force that opposes the relative motion of two or more surfaces in
   contact

FIRE
BREATHING

Those first few acts have you at the edge of your seat. What's next? You watch as a circus performer carries a flaming torch into the center ring. He brings the torch toward his mouth. As he lets out a deep breath, a huge ball of fire erupts. The audience shrieks.

What makes this person a human blowtorch? A fire breather isn't just blowing out air. He has filled his mouth with a **combustible** liquid, a liquid that explodes when it comes into contact with heat. When he breathes, he is spitting out the fluid with his breath. The liquid hits the fire on the torch. The flame bursts into a huge plume. He looks like a dragon from a storybook!

Fire breathing looks super cool, but it's also super dangerous. The performer needs things to happen just right. He must tilt his head at the correct angle. If he tilts it too high, the fire can fall back onto him. If he blows too low, the flame may go straight to the ground. He also has to pay attention to what's happening around him. If he's outside, he has to think about the wind. A strong wind can blow the flame right back into his face. He must also stay a safe distance away from other people.

combustible—capable of easily catching fire and burning

CIRCUS FACT

These spectacular performers are sometimes called "human volcanoes."

GLASS
WALKING

What is this circus planning next? A long bed of broken glass is spread across the ring. A performer begins slowly walking across. It makes you cringe as you hear the shards move under his feet. The man makes it to the other end of the short path. He picks up his feet to show the audience. No cuts. No blood. Is it really glass? Yes. You better believe it!

So why does the performer have no wounds? As he walks, his weight is equally distributed among each piece of glass under his feet. If the performer were to step on only one piece, all his weight would be concentrated on just that piece. It would likely cut through his foot because of the large pressure! But stepping on multiple pieces at a time causes less pain. There is less force concentrated in one area. **Displacement** is also at work here. As the performer walks, one piece of glass may move another. The pieces shift, becoming flatter and easier to walk on.

There are a few more tricks to this trade. These brave performers only use glass broken from large bottles with wide curves. Shards from these bottles have fewer sharp edges. Also, the layout of the glass is important. The bed of glass is thick, but not tightly packed together. This allows displacement to occur more easily. Tiny, more dangerous pieces of glass often fall to the bottom of the pile as well.

displacement—the movement of an object from one position to another

GLOBE OF TERROR

Vroom! Vroom! Vroom! You hear engines revving. Five motorcycle riders enter an enormous steel cage. The cage is shaped like a ball. Seconds later they zoom around the inside of the cage — criss-crossing paths as they go round and round and upside down in the globe of terror. Surely, they are going to crash — but they don't! How can this be?

Centripetal force is at work. It's the force that keeps the bikes moving in a circular path. In this case, it's the upward force on the tires by the inside surface of the globe. Also, when a tire rolls along a dry, solid surface, the surface kind of "grabs" at it. This is friction. It keeps the motorcycle from losing traction. These forces work together to keep the motorcycle's wheels on the inside surface of the ball.

Speed is also important in the globe of terror. The performers must plan the exact speed at which each of them will travel. Once they're all moving, they have to keep the same speed. If one goes much faster or slower than the others, there will eventually be a crash.

DON'T TRY THIS AT HOME

TRY THIS INSTEAD

This simple experiment will show you how centripetal force is at work in the globe of terror. All you need for this experiment is a penny and a balloon. Insert the penny into the balloon. Blow up the balloon until it's about the size of your head. Twist and tie the end. Hold the balloon from the tied end so it's hanging down. Begin to spin the balloon in a circular motion. The penny should begin zooming around the inside of the balloon. This is very similar to the motorcycles in the globe of terror! If you stop moving the balloon, you'll see that the penny temporarily keeps moving.

CIRCUS FACT

The motorcycles inside the ball normally travel between 40 and 60 miles (64 and 97 kilometers) per hour.

KNIFE THROWING

"We need a volunteer," the ringmaster says. A brave young woman walks to the center of the stage. She stands against a wall as a circus performer flings a handful of knives in her direction. *Swish! Swish! Swish!* The knives fly at her. *Thunk! Thunk! Thunk!* They bury themselves into the wall, barely missing her body.

How do performers do this stunt without stabbing the volunteer? These are trained professionals. They know exactly what they are doing. Several science factors help us understand how. First, the performer knows just how hard to throw the knife. The force of the throw determines its initial speed. The knife will miss the target if it's too fast or too slow. The distance between the thrower and the target will determine how much force is needed.

Once the knife is released from the hand, it begins to spin. The angle from which the knife is thrown will determine how much it spins. If it spins too much or too little, the blade won't hit the wall. A knife only spins around once or twice before reaching its target. Sometimes it only makes a half-turn.

Practice is particularly important to this circus act — one wrong move could be disastrous. The performer must develop very good eye-hand coordination. This means his throwing hand has to follow where his eye wants the knife to go. Finally, there is aim. Throwers don't look at the volunteer. Instead, they focus on the parts of the wall that are open.

their hands. They're hanging by their *hair*. Wow!

How come their hair isn't painfully ripping out of their heads? Performers rely on the equal distribution of weight. To distribute something means to spread it around. Hair hang artists weave their hair into long braids. These braids, which act like ropes, are tied to a large steel ring. When the ring is hooked onto the wire, the performer's hair can hold her up. If the braiding is done right, the pull from her weight is distributed evenly around her head. That helps ease the pain and keeps it from yanking out. She won't stay in the air long, either. The longer she stays up, the more pain she will feel.

CIRCUS FACT

Hair hang artists don't use hair products, such as dyes, which can weaken their hair. Instead, they apply special conditioner several times a day. It helps strengthen their hair.

WHEEL
OF DEATH

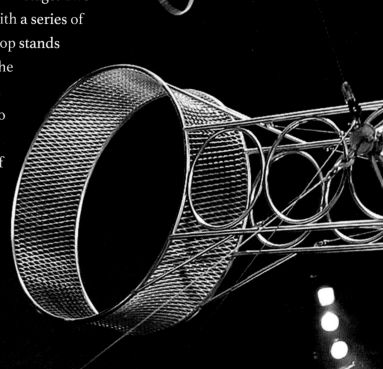

It's the final act of the circus. You know it's going to be a stunner. An enormous contraption is wheeled onto the stage. Two huge hoops are connected with a series of metal beams. Inside each hoop stands a performer. As they move, the contraption begins to rotate. As it spins, the performers do flips and somersaults. One performer even climbs out of his circle to perform stunts on the outside! Behold the wheel of death!

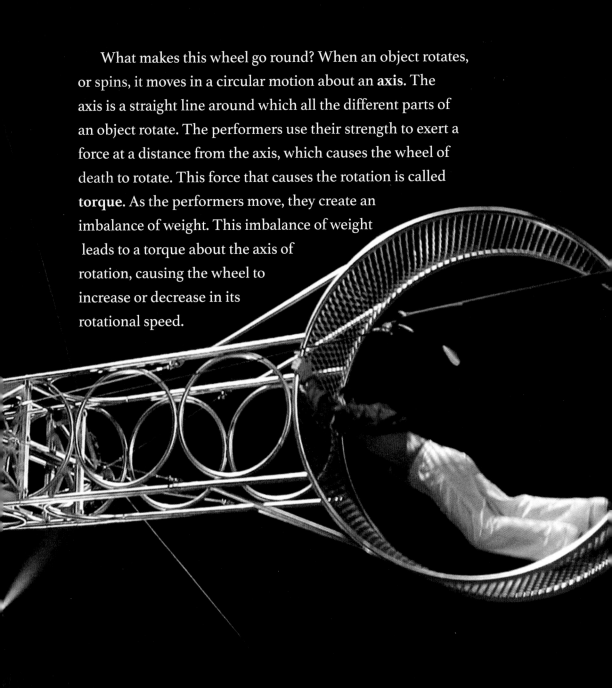

What makes this wheel go round? When an object rotates, or spins, it moves in a circular motion about an **axis**. The axis is a straight line around which all the different parts of an object rotate. The performers use their strength to exert a force at a distance from the axis, which causes the wheel of death to rotate. This force that causes the rotation is called **torque**. As the performers move, they create an imbalance of weight. This imbalance of weight leads to a torque about the axis of rotation, causing the wheel to increase or decrease in its rotational speed.

rotate—to turn in a circle
axis—the straight line around which an object rotates
torque—the tendency of a force to rotate an object about an axis

SAFETY AT THE CIRCUS

Safety is very important to circus performers. Safety keeps these incredible circus acts from becoming deadly. Being prepared for something to go wrong can be the difference between life and death for circus performers. Safety equipment is a must at all circuses.

Safety nets are one example. High-wire walkers, trapeze artists, and human cannonballs are just a few of the performers who rely on safety nets. Safety nets are made of very tough, flexible material such as nylon. Performers can land on the soft net. It slows their fall as it bounces to a stop.

Performers are taught how to land too. In fact, intentionally falling and landing is a part of practice. It helps prepare performers for an accident during a live act. The best way to fall is to land on the back. It spreads the impact throughout the body. If they can't land on their back, then they land on their side or in a "belly-flop" position. Head first, or at a strange angle, can cause serious injury.

SAFETY RIGGING

Aerial artists are often protected by a series of wires. The system of safety wires a circus uses is called **rigging**. The wires are difficult for an audience to see, but they're there. At some circuses aerial artists wear a harness. The harness catches the performer if he or she starts to fall. Although the audience may find this less exciting, it makes the act safer, especially for less-experienced performers.

The most important safety measure is prevention. This is anything that can be done to avoid accidents in the first place. In addition to practice and rehearsals, circus performers are in excellent physical condition. The lighter and more muscular they are, the less likely they are to make a mistake.

CIRCUS FACT

Being a safety inspector is just one of the many jobs at a circus. The safety inspector makes sure all the equipment works right. He or she also figure out ways to make acts safer.

rigging—system of ropes, cables, or chains

GLOSSARY

axis (AK-siss)—the straight line around which an object rotates

center of mass (SEN-tur UVH MASS)—the point in an object around which its mass is evenly distributed

centripetal force (sen-TRI-puh-tuhl FORS)—the force that keeps an object moving in a circular path

combustible (kuhm-BUS-tuh-buhl)—capable of easily catching fire and burning

displacement (dis-PLAYS-muhnt)—the movement of an object from one position to another

esophagus (i-SAH-fuh-guhss)—the tube that carries food from the mouth to the stomach

force (FORS)—an interaction, such as a push or pull, that changes the motion of an object

friction (FRIK-shuhn)—a force that opposes the relative motion of two or more surfaces in contact

gravity (GRAV-uh-tee)—an attractive force that exists between any two objects, including between Earth and everything on it

lubricant (LOOB-rih-kuhnt)—a slippery substance that helps the surfaces of two objects to easily move against each other

pressure (PRESH-ur)—a force exerted on an object over a particular amount of its surface

projectile (pruh-JEK-tuhl)—an object that is shot or thrown through the air

rigging (RIG-ing)—the system of ropes, cables, or chains used for support

rotate (ROH-tate)—to turn in a circle

torque (TORK)—the tendency of a force to rotate an object about an axis

volume (VOL-yuhm)—the amount of space taken up by an object

READ MORE

Doudna, Kelly. *The Kid's Book of Simple, Everyday Science*. Minneapolis: Scarletta, 2013.

Gogerly, Liz. *Circuses*. Explore! London: Wayland, 2017.

Mercer, Bobby. *Junk Drawer Physics: 50 Awesome Experiments that Don't Cost a Thing*. Junk Drawer Science. Chicago: Chicago Review Press, 2014.

Royston, Angela. *Forces and Motion*. Essential Physical Science. Chicago: Heinemann Library, 2014.

Turnbull, Stephanie. *Circus Skills*. Super Skills. Mankato, Minn.: Smart Apple Media, 2013.

INTERNET SITES

Use FactHound to find Internet sites related to this book.

Visit *www.facthound.com*

Just type in 9781515772835 and go.

INDEX